Madam C.J. Walker's
Road
To Success

Written by Donnette Black

Illustrated by Mohamed Qovaiz

Publishing by S.E.E.D.S Publishing.

First published by AuthorHouse 8/14/2010

ISBN: 978-1-4520-2443-1 (sc)

Library of Congress Control Number: 2010911875

Printed in the United States of America

Dedication

This book is dedicated to my two children Samari and Beautiful whom I love dearly. I'd like to first thank Aleia Bundles whom encouraged me, gave me the blessings to write about her great great grand mother and supplied me with the wonderful images in the book THANK YOU you're an incredible woman and writer!

Thank you to Titi and Miko owners of "Miss Jessies" hair products, for all their support! Jerry Brown my editor. Danyelle and Destinye for reading my book drafts about 27,836 times ☺. I'd also like to pay homage to my super women, My Mother Porsha, Grandmother Susie and my Aunt Teresa thank you for your strength, courage and wisdom!

Love Always,
Akua

There was once a phenomenal woman named Sarah Breedlove later known as Madam C.J. Walker. Sarah was a passionate social activist, which is someone who fights for the rights of others. However she is best recognized as the first known African woman born after slavery in America to become a millionaire. She became successful by turning her own personal tragedies into success and using her hardships as strength. Sarah created life changing opportunities for herself by starting her own hair product business! This is how Sarah Breedlove's road to success began....

Sarah's life was hard in the beginning. Born just two days before Christmas on December 23, 1867, long before computers or even televisions were invented. She was raised on a Louisiana slave plantation where her parents were once slaves, but fortunately for Sarah, slavery ended just before she was born. When she was seven years old, her parents died from a common illness at the time called yellow fever. After Sarah's parents died, Sarah and her older sister Louvenia found work doing other peoples laundry, her big brother Alex moved to the next city to find work. Eventually, Louvenia got married and Sarah went to live with them. She did not like living there because her sister's husband was very cruel to her.

When Sarah was only 14, she was excited to marry the man she fell in love with and moved. Even though she'd miss her sister, she was happy to escape her sister's husband. Shortly after marriage, Sarah gave birth to her only child, a beautiful baby girl whom she named Lelia.

Unfortunately, when Sarah was 20 years old, her husband died. Sarah had to be strong since she now had to take care of her daughter and herself. She gathered their things and moved to St. Louis, Missouri, where it was said laundresses like her self made good money. Sarah while working, would spend countless hours bent over a wooden tub scrubbing clothes, starching and ironing. Education was very important to Sarah, so although she only made $1.50 a week, she was determined to save money to one day send Lelia to college. Sarah knew that without college, her daughter would not have many opportunities for a decent paying job. More than likely, she would end up as an under paid house cook, house cleaner or clothes washer which is what many of the women had to do at this time. Sarah did not want that type of work for her daughter.

In 1902, Leila finished high school and Sarah's motivation and persistence paid off with the money she had worked very hard to earn and save she was able to send her daughter to college in Knoxville, Tennessee. A couple of years later, Sarah attended a state fair in St. Louis. It was there that something very inspiring happened; She heard a speech by a woman named Margaret Washington who was the wife of Booker T. Washington, a well known author and educator. As Sarah listened to her speech she watched with admiration. Sarah was fascinated by Mrs. Washington's clothes and her eloquent way of speaking. She was inspired by Mrs. Washington overall. Sarah hoped that she too would have a polished look and dignified presence some day!

Because Sarah did not know how to read and write well she attended night school to learn. There was one big problem for Sarah however... when it came to her appearance she was quite embarrassed. Sarah of course didn't have much money for fancy clothes and over the years Sarah's hair had become very weak and brittle. She was actually balding in some places. Sarah wasn't sure what to do to make her hair grow back. She tried many different products and home remedies but none of them worked, but Sarah refused to quit.

One night Sarah had an amazing dream. It was so colorful and bright. She was walking in Africa and saw beautiful flowers, animals and lots of people doing their daily duties. Then out of nowhere, a man appeared. He told Sarah to mix a few herbs together and her hair would begin to grow again! As time passed, Sarah thought about the dream she had. She decided that with the knowledge of hair care she would try to mix the herbs that the man told her about in her dream.

In 1905, after deciding to save for the items she needed to buy, Sarah received terrible news. Her brother Alex, who was living in Denver with his wife and 4 daughters had died. His death left his wife and four children alone so Sarah moved there to help them out. When Sarah moved, she got a job as a cook for a man who owned the largest pharmacy in Denver. This was convenient because he was able to offer medical suggestions for the hair mix. As Sarah cut and prepared food she often thought about how much closer she was to collecting the money she needed for the special ingredients. Sarah believed that hard work, faith and determination would get you closer to your goals.

Sarah's determination paid off once again! She saved enough money to send for the special ingredients that she needed! Sarah waited patiently for the package to arrive from Africa. It was so far away from The United States of America that the Africans sent the package on a boat because people did not use airplanes for mail back then. A few weeks later, Sarah received the package. She mixed all the special ingredients together and made a cream that she applied to her hair everyday anxiously awaiting the results.

After a few weeks ... Sarah's hair began to grow back! It was

Full,
Healthy
And strong.
It was amazing!

Soon Sarah's hair was growing in faster than it had ever fallen out! She was so excited! Her hair grew all the way back and it was it was even longer and healthier than before.

Just to make sure the cream worked on other people's hair Sarah also applied the cream on her friends and it worked! Her healthy hair made her feel proud. She figured other women would love to have the same prideful feeling and would be willing to buy the hair growing cream from her.

She planned buy more ingredients to make jars of the hair growing cream. That's right; Sarah Breedlove would start her own business! She cooked during the day and at night she strategized her business.

When Sarah moved from St Louis, she kept in contact with a friend named Charles Joseph Walker through mail. Charles moved to Denver six months after Sarah did. He worked for a local newspaper. Charles and Sarah fell in love and in 1906 got married.

It was after getting married that Sarah Breedlove changed her name. This was in the early 1900's and life for most African-Americans was very difficult. Women did not have the same rights as men. During that time, some people called black women 'girls' and Sarah did not like that. She felt as though it was disrespectful to call a grown woman a girl so she changed her name to "Madam C.J. Walker." She wanted people to respect her and call her by a name that held much elegance and grace. They called her Madam Walker or Madam C.J. Walker!

Sarah, now known as Madam C.J. Walker, and her husband Charles Joseph Walker, made the "Madam C.J. Walker Manufacturing Company" and started selling the magical hair cream called "Madam C.J. Walker's Wonderful Hair Grower."

Each container sold for $0.50 cents. She also sold vegetable shampoo and glossine, which was a light oil used to make hair shiny. They put Madam Walker's picture on the box. She even used an ad with a before and after picture of herself to show people exactly how well the products worked! Charles helped with the newspaper ads for her hair growing product. He even made it possible to start excepting mail orders!

These are the original Madam Walker's Wonderful Hair Grower and Tetter Salve hair products.

Madam C.J. Walker began selling her 'Wonderful Hair Grower' mainly in southern states like Louisiana and Arkansas. She worked tirelessly. She sold from house to house and church to church. At the houses she offered women free demonstrations of how to use her products. She washed their hair, applied the grower crème and then styled it. The women loved it!

Most women back then didn't take very good care of their hair and felt as though you had to be rich to have nice hair. Madam Walker proved them wrong! Some women thought Miss Walker didn't like kinky hair because she would at times straighten hair, but that wasn't true at all! Madam Walker liked healthy clean hair. However women chose to style their hair was just fi ne with her!

It was very important to Madam Walker that other women get involved with her business so she taught women how to sell her products. The women were called 'Walker agents.' They always had what she considered a "complete" look, wearing crisp, clean white shirts, long black skirts and manicured nails. Proving again to the women they ran across that you do not have to be wealthy to look presentable and lady like.

Madam Walker's sister Louvenia, Alex's wife and her daughter Lelia, now a college graduate, helped with the business. They made a great team.

Madam Walker started selling other types of products such as hair coloring dye, toothpaste, body soap and even made Madam C.J. Walker make up. She began putting advertisement signs on the sides of buses and bigger displays in window fronts. You could even go to your local store and buy her product. Madam Walker became a household name!

21

In 1908, Madam C.J. Walker moved her business headquarters to Pittsburgh, Pennsylvania. There she opened "Lelia College," her first college, named after her daughter. There the women studying learned how to do things like shampoo, color and style hair. They were called "Hair culturists." Today we call people that do hair beauticians or cosmetologists. Because appearance was important to Madam Walker the women always looked neat, wearing crisp white dresses as uniforms Madam C.J. Walker was very proud of the business she created. Because of her company, thousands of African-American women were able to stop washing clothes and working in the fields, they began working for her, selling hair products, teaching in the college and some of her agent schools.

Madam Walker helped these women earn money to send their children to school, build houses and even start their very own businesses! Madam Walker wanted everyone to be successful! She figured the more business owners the better. They'd be able to offer even more jobs.

Walker Theater

Around 1910, Madam C.J.Walker left Lelia in charge of the business in Pittsburgh and moved the headquarters to Indianapolis, Indiana where there was a great railroad system. She would be able to send out products even faster this way. This move was also great for the men and women in the area because she was able to give lots of them jobs. They mixed and sent products all over the world!

Although Madam Walker was now wealthy, the unfair treatment of Black people in the United States still had not changed. One day, Madam Walker went to the movie theater to buy a ticket and the clerk asked her to pay $0.25 cents although the sign said the tickets were $0.10 cents. When Madam Walker inquired as to why she was being overcharged the lady stated it was because Madam Walker was Black. This really upset Walker because she knew that charging a person more money because of the color of their skin was unfair. Madam Walker began to make plans to build a building downtown that would take up a whole block! She wanted to have a movie theater where anyone could watch movies for the same price! She also wanted her head quarters and factory to be inside the building. Her dreams came true!

After years of dedicated work Madam C. J. Walker became very rich and famous. She became the very first female self-made millionaire in the United States of any nationality! She enjoyed her new life but also shared her wealth. She said: "My object in life is not simply to make money for myself or to spend it on myself. I love to use a part of what I make in trying to help others."

Madam Walker was now wealthy enough to help people in many different ways. She donated to churches, organizations, hospitals, and schools. She made the largest donation to the National Association of Colored Women's fund to purchase the Frederick Douglas house and turn it into a museum. Madam Walker also helped build homes for the elderly, gave scholarships to young omen and educational institutions and assisted the National Association for the Advancement of Colored People (N.A.A.C.P.). In 1913, Madam C.J. Walker and her husband decided to separate but continued to work together.

She had a fabulous townhouse built for Lelia in Harlem, New York. Downstairs from the townhouse there was a hair and nail salon. She also opened up a second college. Around this time Madam Walker began to travel outside of the U.S.A to other countries such as Jamaica, Panama, and Cuba. She also began to give speeches to empower other women to open their own business all over the world!

In 1918, Madam Walker also moved to New York and had a large, beautiful mansion built on the Hudson River. It was a three-story home with 34 rooms. She had extravagant things like a pipe organ used to gently awaken house guests, Persian rugs and hundreds of paintings. It was built by Vertner Tandy, New York's first licensed African-American architect, which is a person that designs and builds houses. It was a fascinating house and still stands today! The house is called, "Villa Lewaro." Madam Walker had such a large mansion built as a symbol as to what black people could achieve through faith, hard work and determination!

Madam Walker's business continued to grow. She was apart of many people's success for the rest of her life. She only lived to be 51 years old, dying in 1919, but her legacy lived on much longer. In 1924 The Walker Theatre was finally built and opened to the public, it was even more incredible than Madam Walker even imagined! There was a ball room for dancing, stages and theatres for movies. Lelia Walker continued to run her mother's company. In 1912 Lelia adopted Fairy Mae Bryant also known as known as Mae Walker whom was a model and assistant of Madam Walker's. Mae was her only child. It was Mae and the other women of the Walker family that kept the business going until the year 1985 when Mr. Randolph purchased the company! Since then they have continued Madam Walker's legacy by selling the products. The Walker family has continued the grand dream of Madam CJ Walker's by keeping The Walker Theater open and making it an even bigger deal in Indiana, where you can watch movies, see music concerts, stage plays and real vintage items from Madam Walker's company!

Madam C.J. Walker

Many women today in our modern century are still inspired by Madam C.J.Walker's innovative skills to create and market their very own products! Companies like "Carol's daughter" and another example are the owners of 'MISSJESSIES.' The sisters, Titi and Miko, were so inspired by Madam C.J. Walker and their very own grandmother Miss Jessie that they started a business selling their own hair line products called 'MISSJESSIES.'

Their products specialize in perfecting curls and waves as well as great hair maintenance! Through lots of dedicated work and faith a business that began in New York is now available worldwide and even has two "MISSJESSIES" salons!

Madam C. J. Walker came from the cotton fields of the South where her family used rainwater to wash their clothes. She not only improved her own life, she helped many American women and several African-American men during some very difficult times! As you see, just like Madam C.J. Walker said.... "If I have accomplished anything in life, it is because I have been willing to work hard. If you Work hard, have faith, and dedicate yourself, you too can be successful in anything you want to do."

Here are some more important Madam C.J. Walker facts!

- Madam C.J. Walker did NOT invent the pressing comb.
- Madam C.J. Walker was inducted into the American Health and Beauty Aids Institute's Hall of Fame in 1999.
- Madam C.J. Walker held a competition among her employees not for the most sales, but for whoever completed the most community service!
- Madam C.J. Walker donated large amounts of money to the NAACP's anti-lynching campaign as well as many other political and social causes!

Photographs of Madam C. J. Walker USPS stamp, vintage Walker tins and ads, and Villa Lewaro from the Madam C. J. Walker Family Archives of A'Lelia Bundles

Pictured here is The Madam Walker Theatre Center in Indianapolis. The Walker Theatre is still open and is a great place to go to enjoy the arts. You can appreciate soulful Music, dancing, comedy and acting!

www.walkertheatre.com

This picture was taken in 1924 in front of Madam Walker's house "Villa Lewaro" during a Walker Beauty Culturists Convention.

This is a picture of the terrace of "Villa Lewaro".

Here are some of the original Madam C.J.Walker ad's.

Beauty
that dares to come closer!

Only honest beauty can give you confidence!

Why go on *pretending?* Why *imitate others*—in vain? Start where Madam Walker starts: *with you as you really are!* Go after the *real* beauty which *all* women have within them. Don't bury it *still deeper* under pasty powders and messy oils.

Only Madam Walker's hair and skin cosmetics are designed to *bring out your own* natural beauty! That's why her wonderful HAIR & SCALP PREPARATION knows no rival (60¢ plus 12¢ tax) . . . why her famous GLOSSINE is the queen of all the *light-bodied* pressing oils (45¢ plus 9¢ tax) . . . why her new VAPOIL (50¢ plus 10¢ tax) is the only *really good* way to cold-curl your hair, pressed or *unpressed,* long or short.

Don't "*just wear*" cosmetics like a fad! Buy the *best.* Discover *your own* REAL *beauty!*

Madam C.J.Walker
HAIR AND SKIN
Cosmetics
WORLD'S FINEST OVER 50 YEARS

If your dealer is temporarily "out," order direct from us. Add 20¢ on cash mail order to avoid C.O.D. costs. (Minimum C.O.D. order: $1 deposit plus postal costs). No tax if for beauty shop use, but send professional address.

ADAM C. J. WALKER MFG. CO. · DEPT. E-454 · INDIANAPOLIS, INDIANA

Even with her hat on...

you'd know she uses **Vapoil**

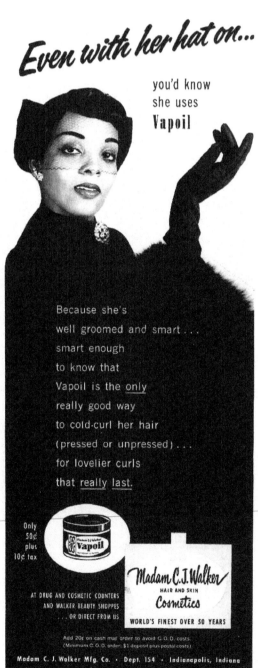

Because she's well groomed and smart... smart enough to know that Vapoil is the only really good way to cold-curl her hair (pressed or unpressed)... for lovelier curls that really last.

Only 50¢ plus 10¢ tax

Vapoil

Madam C.J.Walker
HAIR AND SKIN
Cosmetics
WORLD'S FINEST OVER 50 YEARS

AT DRUG AND COSMETIC COUNTERS AND WALKER BEAUTY SHOPPES ... OR DIRECT FROM US

Add 20¢ on cash mail order to avoid C.O.D. costs. (Minimum C.O.D. order: $1 deposit plus postal costs.)

Madam C. J. Walker Mfg. Co. · Dept. 154 · Indianapolis, Indiana

---

everyone's HEARING about it! .... everyone's TALKING about it!

The one Safe and Certain way to real *Hair Beauty*

HAIR BEAUTY IS SCALP DEEP! When plain hair-dressings only cover up deep-down causes of shabby hair, it really gets worse and WORSE! BEFORE using a dressing, treat itchy or flaking scalp, dandruff or tetter with Madam Walker's DOUBLE-STRENGTH SCALP OINTMENT ... and short, thin, brittle or falling hair by massaging scalp with HAIR & SCALP PREPARATION ... after washing with her SHAMPOO SOAP!

THEN (NOT BEFORE) can you be sure of longest-lasting, silky-soft texture by using GLOSSINE, queen of ALL the light-bodied pressing oils and hair dressings!

BE WISE. Use your head ... for lovely hair!

Madam C. J. Walker Mfg. Co. · Dept. 852 · Indianapolis, Ind.

AT DRUG AND COSMETIC COUNTERS AND WALKER BEAUTY SHOPPES ... OR DIRECT FROM US

GLOSSINE
Only 45¢ Plus Tax
(big beauty shoppe size only $1.25)

DOUBLE-STRENGTH
SCALP OINTMENT Only 60¢ Plus Tax

HAIR AND SCALP
PREPARATION Only 60¢ Plus Tax

TEMPLE SALVE Only 45¢ Plus Tax

Madam C.J.Walker
HAIR
Cosmetics
WORLD'S FINEST FOR 50 YEARS

FOR PERFECT HAIR ATTENTION DON'T FORGET YOUR NEARBY WALKER BEAUTICIAN!

POSTAGE PREPAID ONLY ON CASH ORDERS · NO TAX IF FOR BEAUTY SHOP USE

Photographs of Madam C. J. Walker USPS stamp, vintage Walker tins and ads, and Villa Lewaro from the Madam C. J. Walker Family Archives of A'Lelia Bundles

Madam C.J. Walker's Road To Success

Written by
Donnette Black

Illustrated by
Mohamed Qovaiz

CPSIA information can be obtained
at www.ICGtesting.com
Printed in the USA
BVOW07s2152261217
503583BV00004B/35/P